# Initiate: A Journey Begun

*A Poetry Collection –*
*for the curious*

By
## Neil Axtell

Copyright © 2026 Neil Axtell

# TABLE OF CONTENTS

# DEDICATION

To Johanna, Mia & Edward, who have taught me so much about life and love.

To Jo, Cat, Sarah & Eleanor who helped bring this to life.

# ACKNOWLEDGEMENTS

In memory of Huw Evans who taught me the importance of "just turning up".

Original illustrations by the talented hands of Jennifer Litts

S. D. G.

# About the Author

Living on the outskirts of Cambridge, UK Neil has been writing Poetry seriously for over 10 years. He describes himself as "Husband, Christian, Dad, Engineer, Poet, fixer of things and restorer of others – but not necessarily in that order."

Neil writes in the free verse style – sorry, not a rhyme in sight. He tends towards more long-form "micro stories" where characters come and go but with no back-story. Filling in the blanks is left up to the reader and their imagination.

Neil is married to Johanna, and they have two grown-up children.

# ABOUT THIS BOOK

Firstly, thanks for picking up/buying this book and reading this introduction to my first printed poetry collection.

I've found writing this introduction harder than writing my poems. After reading a number of other book introductions to try and find out "how to do it" I was not much wiser so I've decided to do it my own way – which sums up this collection pretty well too!

I have had an up and down relationship with my writing for many years, often discounting myself and what I write as not being "proper" poetry. This led to a major kick-start in 2016 when I started to take my writing seriously again and stopped comparing myself with others (comparison is a creativity killer). How I write is how I write and I'm not going to try and make it sound like anyone else any more. I appreciate that my writing style will not be to the liking of everyone, but I feel it is more important to be honest to yourself and what has been laid on your heart than anything else.

My writing is largely inspired by my journey of faith as a Christian. In no way does this mean that I think I've "got it" – far from it! Rather, I would like to invite you to walk a while alongside me and share the journey. I hope you will feel able to join me on this journey even if you don't identify yourself as a Christian. All I would ask is that you approach my writing with an open heart and mind.

I describe my writing style as a hybrid form, as it shares aspects of free verse and Poetic Prose. One thing you will notice quite quickly is that many of my poems are longer than a single page. I call my poems "micro stories" because most of them do tell a story or part of a story. I have become comfortable that my poems often don't tell a whole story and probably leave a lot of questions unanswered. I think that it is often in the not-knowing and the unanswered questions that we gain the greatest enjoyment. Each poem will probably resonate in a different way for each reader as it interacts with the imagination and different lived experience of each one.

From the very start I wanted this project to be a collaboration. It has been a real joy to work with visual artists to create the pictures that accompany a number of the poems.

You will also quickly notice that another unusual feature of these poems is that each one has a small "Biography" after it. This gives you as the reader/listener an insight into what prompted me to write the poem in the first place. I have kept these in because all the feedback I've had is that people like to read the "back story" behind each poem – I hope that you do too.

The COVID-19 pandemic and my wife's subsequent significant health challenges injected a significant delay into this project. I am glad that, at last, it has made it to publication.

If you like what you read you can find more on my Substack:
https://throughthestatic.substack.com

# FOREWORD

Writing this foreword and commending to you this book of poems is a such a joy for me and something I am honoured to have been asked to do.

As a friend of Neil's, I have had the huge privilege of sharing some of his recent journey as an emerging Poet and am therefore delighted that he has reached this milestone of publishing his work.

In this fast- paced world we live in, reading through Neil's work is an experience to be savoured and enjoyed slowly. Beautifully crafted, each poem is a delight to read and together they are like a rich tapestry; woven with multiple colours, stories and testimonies that have been drawn from Neil's own life experiences and walk with God.

In reading this book you therefore find yourself not just reading words on a page but responding to a Heavenly Father who knows each one of us and loves to speak to us in unique and creative ways. This, I believe, has been Neil's heart for this collection of his poems and I am personally so thankful that he has so bravely now taken this step to share them with us.

Joanne Maynard
Worship 24/7 Directoress, High Wycombe, UK

# You Are Unique

You are not a mistake, an accident.
You are unique.
You are hand-crafted.
You have a unique relationship with me.

In all of time there has only ever been one you,
and there only ever will be.
Your creative abilities are unique.
The way you interact with me, hear from me, is also
unique.

No single person can fully understand me,
or have a full and complete view of who I am.
I am a far greater mystery than that.

Therefore, the collective needs the views and
understanding of everyone - even you.
Only through everyone bringing their
own creative insight, their own unique insight,
will anything like a full picture of me be revealed.

So, do not hold back!
The creative abilities I have placed within you,
your unique abilities, need to come forth.
Otherwise the collective of my body
will be the poorer without it.
Do not discount yourself or the
skills you have in your hands.

These I have given to you for a purpose.
Don't worry about the end result - that is my concern.
All that I ask of you work together with me
to make the most of those tools, skills, abilities and
capabilities I have put within you.

Only you can do what you do.
You are approved my me.
You don't need approval from anyone else
to do what you do.

*Whilst working on a course about Creativity and its supernatural source/implications, I encountered this theme of our uniqueness and alongside that the killer that is comparison.*

*God, in all his vast creativeness (just look up at the night sky) never runs out of inspiration. He never gets bored. He never gets tired. So, when he created us it was out of joy not compulsion. Nor was it an accident. Neither does God believe in "Cookie-cutter" or "batch production" people.*

*Instead we have literally been lovingly hand-crafted for a specific purpose and to bring our unique understanding of and perspective on our creator. No one person can fully understand God (A. W. Tozer) so we need each other because everyone brings a unique understanding of and insight into God's character. It is only by bringing the collection of these unique insights and experiences together that we get to a wider understanding of and appreciation of God's nature. We need each other. Everyone has something to bring to the party.*

# CONFESSIONS OF A NON-CONFORMIST POET

Dear Reader.
Some say that what I write is not poetry.
That it does not conform to the norm.
That it is not verse but prose.

True, verse it is not as there is no rhyme.
No rhyme within me,
no rhyme on paper.

Sorry.
That is not how my brain is wired.

Others say that it is Poetic Prose and so should conform
to the "rules" of that form. The form where the sentence
is King and line breaks banished, as if they were some
deviant thing. Something to be outcast to the bad lands
to make way for the new enlightenment.

But what is poetry exactly?
Can anyone really define it?
Is it something that can be captured, analysed,
catalogued and defined?
Is it the form that gives it it's being or
the ideas it presents and the emotional response
it engenders and prompts in you dear Reader?

You see, I have a problem.
I have the ideas and images that flow from my pen.

But…

I also like to play with the lines.

To
make
you
pause
and
slow
down.

Rather than skimming your way through
my words and the pictures they paint,
the stories they tell,
as if they were a set of instructions or
Terms and conditions.

I
Want you
To slow down
And **read** my words.

Let them seep into your soul and be
slow-cooked by your imagination.
To become a marvellous rich stew of ideas.

So, I declare myself a proud non-conformist!
I cannot be constrained by the block of text of Prose
Poetry; where the sentence rules as King and the line
break is banished.

I cannot rhyme either.
To contort my ideas into unnaturally short lines
to meet the demands of the final word.
To mangle syntax in the search of lyricism.
I shall leave that to others more skilled and cleverer
than I.

I like playing with the form of my writing on the page.

      Sometimes
            it paints its
                  own picture.

In a world of the 10-second attention span,
I will not treat you like a goldfish dear Reader.

You are called to a much higher order.

Instead, my untidy sentences, those that refuse to keep
themselves short, will sprawl and be
randomly split by semi-intentional line breaks.

Then sometimes I will deliberately
make my lines short.

To use the visual and mental carriage return
of the line break to slow you down dear Reader.
To give you space to think rather
than just consume.

To become active in the exchange of ideas, not passive.

You are worth the extra seconds.

So, conformity be damned!
Form be overlooked!
Rather, read my words to find my heart.

It is worth the investment.

*Reading your poetry publicly always contains an element of risk.*

*I wrote this poem partly out of frustration towards those people who listen to my poems and proceed to critique the form rather than trying to understand the heart and motivation behind it.*

*These criticisms lead to a number of weekends in my own study of poetic forms. I was trying to quell the seed of doubt that had been put in my mind by those who questioned whether what I write is even poetry – "It's just prose isn't it?".*

*After a number of weekends searching online and reading two rather daunting books on Poetic Prose I've now come to a place a peace about what and how I write.*

*Yes, my style breaks a number of "rules" that attempt to classify poetic forms and hence it does not easily sit in one of these pre-defined poetic forms. I have tried to write in Poetic Prose (which strangely for the disruptive, "new kid on the block" status it appears to have, actually has a number of very rigid rules itself) but all the feedback I have received is that my original unconventional layout actually made it easier to read.*

*So, I have now come full circle and taken to heart the wise words of a good friend of mine. She reminded me that my poems are my own art-form and don't need to look like that of anyone else. As I am unique so will my creative expression be.*

*Some may not like it and may disregard it, but I offer it to you dear Reader in its honest form which is now at peace with itself.*

*You may not like what or how I write but that is fine. I offer it with an open hand.*

# SUNRISE

As I sit here, dew on my feet,
In the quiet of early morn,
I just want to sit and enjoy the warm caress
Of the dawn and the early sun.

As it rises into the sky it's
fingers of warmth banish the
cold and dark of night.

They warm my soul.

If I choose to linger in the moment,
as the gentle warmth drives out
the vestiges of sleep and the
fuzziness of dreams,
so you remind me of your love to me.

It is new every morning.

It is as regular and un-ending as the sunrise.
I look forward to the warm touch
of your love as I do the early sun.
Your love should be too hot for
me to handle, like the noon day sun
in the height of summer.

It should burn me up – so imperfect am I.
But instead it renews, assures,
for you do not see me as I do.

When you look on me it is with the eye of love.
The love a father has for their child.
For when you look on me you do not see
all the mistakes and muck and rubbish.
You see me spotless and perfect and your heart rises.

For you see me through your son.
He who really rises like the morn sun.
He who is as reliable as the sun.
He who renews me like the sun.

So I will linger a while in the dawn-day sun.
I will appreciate it's warmth a while.
And give thanks.
That your love Lord does indeed rise every morning.
And as I linger, the sun warming my toes,
I hear a whisper.

"I love you."

*I wrote this poem early one morning at Newday 2016.*

*I had got up to do the washing up from the night before. No-one else on site was stirring. I sat down facing into the early morning sun as I waited for the kettle to boil. Then I heard God say to me "Please go back into your tent, and bring out your pen and notebook". But Lord I said — I've just sat down and I need to do the washing up otherwise we will have nothing to eat breakfast off of. Then I heard/sensed his reply "I know that, but please go back into your tent, and bring out your pen and notebook".*

*As God had been impressing on me over the week that he really wants me to do what he asks me and to do it when he asks me I obeyed and went back into my tent to collect my notebook and pen.*

*So the washing up was a little delayed — but still ready before breakfast!*

# DANCING IN THE SHADOWS

Within minutes of the music striking up
she can contain herself no longer.
Feeling constrained and hemmed in by the
chairs around her, she makes her excuses and
quietly makes for the sanctuary of the
shadows at the back of the hall.

And here she finally feels free to express her
true self as she starts to dance.
As she dances she stops thinking about
what others may think of her and the way
she chooses to express herself.
Hiding in the anonymity the shadows give her,
she's only happy when she's dancing.

She stays in the shadows because she does
not want anyone to see who she really is,
lest she should be judged improper.

But something that cannot be quenched
compels her to express herself.
When she dances nothing else matters.
She is truly lost in the moment.
Lost in her movement expression.
Something that speaks more to her
and about her than simple words ever can.

Movement and expression that links
heart to heart and Spirit to Spirit.
Something that re-establishes eternal communication.
She does not see that while she dances
someone unseen dances with her,
mirroring her every move.

Someone that has followed her into her shadows,
nowhere is off limits to them.
They have freely, willingly left the crowd
to follow the one.
The one of immense worth,
incalculable value.
The one that was and is missed.

She dances in the shadows because comparison
has made her its unwitting slave.
Instead of following her unique and beautiful path
she has attempted to follow the paths of others.
To make her footprints fit into the footprints of others.
To make her normal stride fit that others.
To deny her true self.

She thinks she has nothing new to bring.
Her view of herself has become engulfed
with her failures.
Instead of taking his hand and dancing her
unique dance with him, she had traded
it for a pale pastiche.

She fails to see that she has been painstakingly
and purposefully made for a unique
relationship and purpose with him.

Fashioned with incredible care and attention,
the passions and gifts that have been placed
within her are intended to create a unique
contribution to life and love.

A unique signpost to him.

*This poem came about during a short worship session at the beginning of a small group meeting at my local church. I have to admit that during this Covid-19 pandemic season I've found trying to do corporate worship over a Zoom call not a wonderful experience. As I was musing on this the idea for this poem came to my mind.*

*It sometimes feels that we've been 'conditioned" in church life to regard some forms of creative expression more appropriate for times of worship than others. Someone even went so far as to ask whether we had put sung worship on some sort of pedestal and regard it as the only "proper" way to worship God in a corporate setting.*

*I don't believe that is right. God is an infinitely creative being and has created each one of us uniquely. Therefore, it should be little surprise if we all have a unique creative response in worship. Trying to force everyone into the same worshipful "box" only means we miss out as a collective body.*

*I know quite a few people who feel happiest when expressing their worship through movement. Unfortunately, many feel that they can only do this at the back of a church meeting. Not because they need to space (though this may sometimes be a consideration) but because they don't feel that what they are doing will be accepted. Hence, they are literally "dancing in the shadows". As I was pondering on this I had a clear picture of God joining them in their dance to him in the shadows.*

*So, to everyone who expresses themselves through movement, please don't feel contained and constrained by prison of chairs around out. Step out and freely express your love to Him who made you.*

28

# The Word

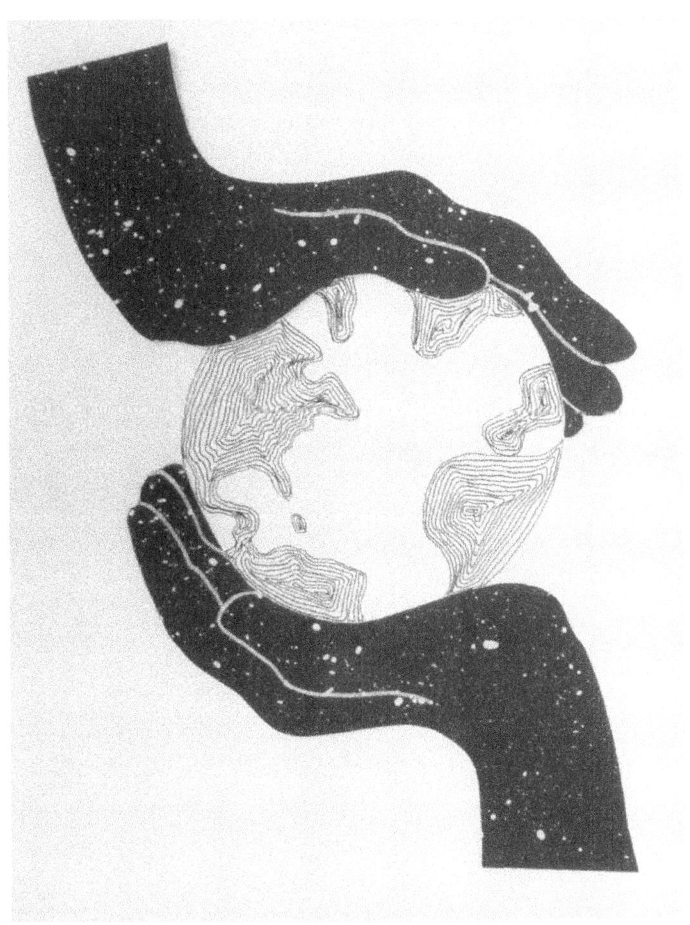

*Image credit – Jennifer Litts sdg*

# THE WORD

Before there was you were.
The Word one with the Father.
A word was whispered into the void and
darkness was replaced with light.
Light in its countless millions of worlds.
Arrayed in the night's sky like a necklace of iridescent
gems.

But the Word did not stop.
He co-laboured with the Father and Spirit
on the wondrous mystery.
The Word spoke it all.
The Word saw it all.
Nothing that is was without him.

The stars started their dance through the heavens,
stretching their canopy above the Earth.
Raising his tent above all those dwelling below.

As the earth started to spin so the
orchestrated ballet played out in the sky above.
For even without the sun there was light
and beauty
and testament.

As the eons rolled past, like waves on the sand,
the Word continued to be, to act and to speak.
As the empires of man rose and fell
so the Word brooded over them all.
All seeing, all knowing, all creating.

As man's hands created and crafted,
little did they know the guiding Word.
But in all their creativity the sons of man rarely
acknowledged nor recognised the creator.
However, a very few did.
A few felt his breath, his guidance and
became bearers of the message.
But over time even these fell silent.

So the Word, the Chi-Rho, that which was there
when time first ticked became willingly
constrained by it.
Direct intervention was now required.
No more messengers.
The creator became one of the created.
The creator became completely dependent
on those he had created.

One of the stars the Word had made
was used to announce the event.
Announced not to the great and the good,
but to the humble and humble of heart.
Many visitors came from near and far and
marvelled at the scene.
The Word become flesh.

Gifts were bestowed.
Given to the one who was and is and is to come.
Gifts that reflected the truth of the now and
the reality of that which was yet to come.
Through all this a young maiden looked on and
gathered and treasured these events in her heart.

By this act the Word came down and
pitched his tent with us and over us.
Through this he dwelt with us and we
communed with him,
whether we recognised him or not.

But even at that tender age death stalked the Word
and attempted to overcome it.
So into exile he went, becoming a
refugee in a foreign land.
Following the footsteps of many before him.
Leading a way that many down the ages would follow.

The rhythm of the seasons marked time.
For one score years and ten, the Word
walked and worked amongst us.
Then came the time for the Word
to become proactive once again.

But in this upside-down Kingdom the Word eschewed
the self-righteous and self-important.
Instead, revealed himself to those who
knew of their need the most.
To those ignored by society or
considered of little worth.

The invisible people.
The Word came not to groups or tribes or nations,
but to the individual.
The co-creator meeting with the created.

The subversive message of the
upside-down Kingdom became
too much for those with vested interests.
Those with earthly power they were
desperate to cling to.
So truth and justice were discarded and the Word
was tried and convicted by the created.

The problem had to be eradicated
so that the norm could be preserved.
And so, with the washing of hands execution was
both sanctioned and ordained.
Just one more potential uprising to be crushed.
A required act to persist the status-quo.

And as the Word fell silent,
as heaven became impenetrable,
the sun closed its eyes and cried.
Tears that mirrored those of a mother for her son.
The stars also looked away from this scene of injustice.
The earth itself trembled.

Darkness came to claim what it thought was owed.
But the Word remembered the time before time.
Darkness could not prevail.
Instead, the veil that stood between God and man
was torn asunder.

The Word shouts his name over us from heaven.
Over those he has called as his own.
From his throne in heaven the Word roars

But to those the Word calls he calls with a whisper.
The Word calls from the quiet place.
As it did to Mary in the garden.
The Word addresses us by name and
we recognise his voice.
Amazed that he should and does know us.
Regards us.
Looks over us.
Loves us.

As it was at the beginning, in the Word is life.
This life is the light of mankind.
The true light which enlightens everyone.
Through his invitation we get to share his light.
To work together with the Word.
To work together with the Father.
To work together with the Spirit.

Through this labour a little piece of heaven
is brought down to earth.

*This poem came about in an unusual way for me. Usually I have either a word, picture or series of pictures that kickstarts the creative process. Not in this case. Instead God drew me to the beginning of John 1. I ended up writing out John 1 v1 – 5 from a number of translations and reading them over and over again.*

*Next came the writing process itself. This was also unusual for me too. Usually I write the first draft of my poems longhand from beginning to end in one session. Not this time. God kept on giving me small snippets/paragraphs one at a time over a period of about 2 months. Sometimes I would ask "Is that all Lord?" to be told to simply be patient and wait. The paragraphs also did not come in the final order. It was only once I had transcribed all the disassociated paragraphs from my notebook (yes an old fashioned, physical paper notebook) into the word processor did the final order and flow of the poem become evident.*

*Yes, this is a long poem but it does have to convey a rather long story! I hope that it gives you a new insight into the marvellous story we are part of and the active part we each have to play. There are no extras in this story.*

# DESERT OASIS

The vast desert stretches before me.
It fills my vision from horizon to horizon.
Bronze-yellow undulating dunes
flow one into another as far as I can see.

By day the sun blazes down
and bakes the sand beneath my feet.
I feel its heat coming up through my shoes.
Each step clings to my leaden feet.
The wind stirs up the sand and flings it into my face,
stinging my cheeks and blinding my eyes.

By night the warmth of the sun is replaced
by the chill of its silver sibling the moon.
Despite my cloak the cold of night gnaws at my bones
and sleep eludes me.

The landscape changes only slowly.
Direction is hard to find.
Day repeats night, repeats day repeats night.
A day feels like the one that preceded it.
I feel I am making no headway.

Then one day a smudge appears on the horizon.
Something that stands upright.
Something that interrupts the
smooth line of the horizon.
With each passing day it grows taller,
until at last I recognise it's signpost. Oasis!

More days of travail pass by. Then in the
lengthening shadows of late afternoon I arrive.
Arrive at this island of cool and plenty
amongst the sea of heat and sand.
I rush and bury my head in the cool sweet water,
letting its refreshment pass over me.

When I surface I notice that I am also no longer alone.
I see a tent, smell a fire and hear a crackling.
Its inhabitant hails me
"Welcome friend! You look like a man in need of
refreshment!"

Indeed, I do.

I am ushered to an exotic rug laid out on the
sand in front of the fire.
Soft cushions are arrayed to make me comfortable.
"Come, come" says my host "join me for some tea".
Above the crackling fire sits a kettle.
Gently hissing and bubbling to itself.
They reach over, pour its contents into a pot and,
after a time, hands me a cup of the sweet drink.

It is nectar to my parched throat.
"Drink, enjoy, rest!" implores my host with a smile.
As the dark gathers once more its creeping cold
tries to encircle me – but this time to no avail.
Here, with my new friend, in front of their fire,
I am safe and warm.

"You must be hungry – here eat" and without a
second thought my host shares their food with me.

As the night deepens, the stars twinkle into sight
as the embers from the fire seem to take flight,
leaping into the sky to try and join the stars.
The night passes slowly as my new-found friend
and I lie back and study the magnificent show above.

We talk of many mysteries.
Day follows night follows day once more.
But my host shows no sign of moving on
and their generosity continues.
My needs are met without request.

Who am I to them?
What can I bring?
What can I say?
What can I do?

Then one day I see another sight on the horizon.
The wisp of a dust trail.
The footprint of the traders camel train.
I hesitate.
I feel drawn but do not wish to leave.
Suddenly my new friend is at my shoulder,
also studying the horizon.
"You need to leave don't you?" they ask.
"Yes – but I don't want to" I reply.
"I know – but if you stay you will never
know what wonders await."

The next day, at break of dawn I leave my oasis home.
Head out once more into my nemesis, the desert.
To find the camel train I see in the distance before me.

I cannot tarry any more. I am drawn forever onwards.

*This, rather longer than expected, poem attempts to explain what it feels like to me when you come across that right person at the right time who encourages you onward. You may never meet them again but for that moment they were God's right person in the right place at the right time.*

*I started the process of sharing my poems in 2016. At times it has felt like walking through a desert because I've struggled to find any people local to me who use similar creative expression. Sharing via the Internet can be a strangely lonely experience because you rarely get any feedback. For me it would be great to have people alongside me as I continue to see where God wants to take me on this particular journey.*

*At NewDay 2017 I bumped into one such person. So, Cat C. if you ever get to read this you were God's right person in the right place at the right time for me. You've given me the encouragement to carry on.*

*I suspect all of us go through "desert times" in our Christian life. So if this rings true for you I pray that you too will come across that right person in the right place at the right time. However, and whoever you identify with the host at the oasis in this poem I hope you meet them soon. Much as we may want to stay in the moment, sometimes they will just be people who pass through our lives.*

*Since writing this several people have asked me who the mysterious host is in this poem. Well, I have left it deliberately ambiguous because they will mean different things to different people at different times.*

# CRONUS – A LAMENT

*Image credit – Jennifer Litts sdg*

# CRONUS – A LAMENT

You called me to spend two hours alone
with you my Lord.
They felt as intimidating as this blank page.
What could I possibly have to say for two hours!
What would you want to say to me?
But still you invited me to a quiet place
to spend time with you.

Forgive me for my unbelief and lack of faith.
The lack of faith that my God and my Lord would not
do what he said he would do.
My unbelief that he who died for me, in my place, and
now calls me his friend
would not want to spend time with me.

Oh Lord I want to know your heart.
To be able to distinguish your voice in
all the babble of everyday life.
Because you whisper to me.
You do not shout or raise your voice.

Most of the time I just walk on by.
I do not choose to accept your invitation
to stop and rest awhile.
I choose not to tune my heart with yours and hence
I do not hear your voice calling to me.

Oh Lord I am so fickle.
I love it when I sense your presence and
when I hear your voice.

But I choose to make these times few and far between.
Forgive me for I still have much to learn.
To discern your voice, your prompting
and to linger awhile with you.

I have been bought with a price.
A life for a life.
I am fit only to be your servant.
But you desire and declare me your friend!

Oh that I, a wretched sinner, should be declared
a friend of the most high!
The one who was with God when the universe
sparked into existence.
The one under who's feet all principalities and powers
have been placed.
The one who sits at the right hand of God.
It is he that declares to the whole world
that he is my friend.
It is you.

Oh my Lord. Help me to love you more and more.
To delight in those times when you come to visit.
Prevent me from ignoring you as you gently tap.
Leaving you outside the door to my life.
The door to my heart.

Oh my Lord please give me once again
the ability to see pictures.
Reveal once again to me understanding
about what I see.
Help me once again to write of you my God, my King,
but most of all my friend.

Help me to express the little I know of you to others,
so that they too may come in from the cold.
Help me introduce them to the
thawing warmth of your love,
so that you can draw them into the light from the
freezing dark.

Oh my Lord, my friend.
I know you chose the weak things so that
your strength may shine out.
I thank you that any good in me is because of your
friendship.
But sometimes, maybe most of the time, I feel too weak.
I get it wrong so many times.

Help me, my friend, to fight my daily battles
and overcome.
Send your Holy Spirit to guide me and
give me strength.
Give me your gift of faith so that I can be sure
of that which I do not know
and have hope in that which has not yet happened.

Help me on my journey.
You have called me from the lush, green,
pleasant summer river valley.
From the peace and quiet of the river and the trees
upwards to the barrenness of the mountain.
As I start this trek and look back on
that which I leave behind,
I am so thankful that, even though I appear alone,
my holy friend is with me.

You have done so much for me.
You did not even stop at dying for me.
But not only this, as if this was insufficient,
you have given me eternal life
and friendship with you.

You have promised to be with me always.
I know that you will never ask me to do something for
which you will not supply the resources.
Please just give me strength when I forget.
The ability to stop the world when you come calling.

*Whilst hunting in the loft/attic for some of our kid's books I came across some old notebooks of mine. In one of them was this rather longer than usual poem. I did dither a bit about whether or not I should publish it but two things have made me do so.*

*What I write is about my walk through the Christian life. It's the only one I can write about. If I only write about the highs and not the lows then I am not being truthful. I am only describing half a life. As my friends know, honesty is important to me and so I have shared some very personal poems which some may have kept private. I've shared these because I feel God prompting me to share about my whole life of faith – the good bits and the bad bits. The Bible is full of stories of people of faith going through tough times and so we should not be afraid to tell our stories of times of struggle. It is often through the times of struggle that God works because we are more dependent on him. As a great friend of mine so wisely observed, "Being a Christian does not mean that we are immune from the ups and downs and challenges of life, they will still happen. The difference is that we know we are not facing them alone". It also reinforces the truth that God does not wait until we are perfect before intervening in our lives. Rather, he intervenes when we are at our most imperfect, when we have turned our back on him and don't even recognise our need of him. If we only ever write about the good times in our faith journey, then it can make it seem that you have to have achieved some sort of saint-like degree of perfection before God will even consider entering into a relationship with us. The reality is entirely the reverse, so I write (I hope) about the lows as well as the highs and the times I struggle. It is all about being real.*

*The second reason for publishing this came about after a brief conversation with a good friend of mine at church. I was telling them about these old poems I had found and that at least one of them was sort of like a lament. Their reply was "Well I think we could do with more laments." which really got me thinking. When we read the Psalms there is plenty of lamenting going on as there is in many of the stories from the prophets. So why do we hesitate to publish them now? Maybe we feel that everything has to be perfect or to admit that everything is not perfect somehow makes us a lesser Christian or someone "lacking faith".*

*As I read the New Testament I don't see Jesus promising us that our life here on earth will be perfect. Rather I see that it will be full of challenges but we know that we do not travel through these times alone and that eventually we will overcome. The journey we take with him is more important many times that the destination we get to.*

# THE ICE MAIDEN

She knew the names they called her.
Never to her face, but muttered and whispered.

The more waspish in the harbour called her "uncan" -
meaning "from another area".
All the names they used reinforced
that she was a stranger.
One kept at arm's length.
The untrusted.

Her looks betrayed her Nordic heritage.
Long, straight blonde hair hung like a curtain
in front of her face, hiding her pale blue eyes.
Not that anyone ever looked her in the face.

Eyes were always averted, streets crossed.
If anyone had looked they would have seen
eyes of such a pale blue they almost froze your soul.

For her part this loneliness was now to her a friend.
Almost a comfort.
She hardly even saw those around her any more,
they passed like half-seen ghosts.

She kept herself to herself.
Kept herself away from any more hurt.
Trust no-one.
Rely on no-one.
Love no-one.

She only had two refuges in life.
Her tiny house and the coffee shop.
Not a well-known, brash chain emporium,
but small, independent, tucked out of the way.
A shop always visited when she knew
it would be empty.
When no-one would try and interact.
When she could retreat to the smallest table
in the corner.

Back to the wall she was safe.
A book her only companion.
Earphones shut out the rest of the unwelcoming world.

Then one evening her world was thrown into disarray.
Invaded.
This time all the tables were taken.
Others were here.
And in her redoubt,
her castle amongst the aromas of steam and coffee.
Her refuge.
Her citadel.
Her sanctuary.
There was another.

Sat in her spot.
Sat with his back to the wall.
She felt the panic rising.
There was nowhere "safe" to sit in this tiny place.
This stranger had invaded her routine.

She stood transfixed.
Unable to go forward.
Unable to go back.

Then the stranger did something no-one
had done for a very long time.
He looked up.
Looked her straight in the face, and smiled.
Looked her in the eye and smiled.

But still she was transfixed.
Her inner turmoil only increased when he said
"I'm sorry, I've sat in your seat."
"But there is an empty one opposite me."
"I hate to drink alone."
"You could join me."

He motioned to the chair in front of him.
She felt herself moving,
walking towards the invited chair.

And then she was sitting down.
Looking into a face that almost felt familiar.
Then she gasped as she realised something else.
"I see you!" she whispered.
For indeed she could.
Whilst all others wafted around her
like half-seen spectres,
this man was as clear as looking at herself.

So, stumbling at first, she entered into something
that had become alien to her.
A conversation.
And as they spoke she realised something else.
He asked few questions.
Yet he knew her.

He knew her comings and goings.
He knew the thoughts that went through her mind.
He knew her hurt.
He knew her ghosts of the past.
He knew of the well of tears inside.
He knew her self-imposed isolation.

In this intimate exchange time slowed.
Slowed right down.
Until reality rudely asserted itself once more
through the stacking of chairs
and the sweeping of floors.

She did not want to leave this encounter.
She wanted it to continue.
To linger.
But her friend, no longer a stranger, stood up.
"I'm sorry, but my time has come."

She stood to try and block his way.
To recapture the moments.
To stay in the moment.

Expecting the familiar rejection,
tears of frustration formed.

Instead she was met by a warm embrace.
Something that triggered memories of long ago.
Something that took her breath away.
Something that made her gasp.
And the tears silently fell,
but for an entirely different reason.

As well as the embrace he left her with a
whispered parting gift - "Believe."

*The inspiration for this poem was again a picture of an individual and an alternative view on how Jesus' conversation with the Samaritan woman at the well may have gone in a 21st century setting.*

*The word "uncan" is a real word. It is part of the Shetland dialect.*

# NORTHERN LIGHTS

*Image credit – Jennifer Litts sdg*

# NORTHERN LIGHTS

It was late afternoon when I came upon this beach.
The golden sands and iridescent waters a
surprise at this latitude.
Discarding shoes I felt the warm sand squeezing
between my toes as I walked along
the high-water mark.
The demarcation between that
which is regularly inundated
and that which remains forever dry.

Sitting on a small, sandy headland where grass
clings to an existence and the Marram grass
fringes the edges,
I watched the sun make its daily rendezvous
with the horizon.

The heat of midday was replaced by
lengthening shadows
and a gentler, golden warmth.
As the sun lost its fight with the horizon,
it slipped from sight.
The sky was transformed from bright blue,
Through shades of amber and red to purple.

And with the approaching night the stillness comes.
The babble of day is replaced with muted tones
and alien sounds that carry much further.

Even the waves modify their pace.
The relentless crashing of the daytime
stills into a much gentler rendition.
Less crashing and more burbling as if
exhausted by the travails of the day

But still they mark time.
A regular heartbeat of the earth.
Now that the sun has slipped its earthly coils,
the cool of night comes to take its place.
From the driftwood I make a fire.
A small facsimile of the now distant sun.

As the wood crackled and the flames continued
their mesmerising yellow dance the stars came out.
They had always been there, I could just not see them.

Then, slowly at first, a new dancer joined this scene.
Iridescent fingers of green flashed into sight
and then disappeared.

Slowly the fingers became bigger and stayed longer,
until they eventually joined together into one
long, undulating curtain of dancing light.
It moved as if provoked by unseen children
playing hide-and-seek behind its ethereal folds.

The Scientists tell me this is just the result of
ionised particles hitting the high atmosphere.
But I think there is a higher orchestrator.

By now a kettle had appeared a-top my fire,
to harness the heat and make a golden brew
that in turn would chase away the chill of night
amid the regular heartbeat of waves.
"That's a beautiful scene isn't it?"
says the stranger who silently appears beside me.
"It does that even if we are not here to see it." they add.

And so the stranger and I sit together and share a brew
as we watch nature's ballet perform in the sky above us.
Few words are exchanged.
Few words need to be exchanged.
We are comfortable in each other's presence.

"You know that I'm always here don't you?"
they ask, eventually.
"I know – yes, but don't always feel." I reply.
"Indeed, and that is why sometimes
you need to see as well."
"But not all the time."

"The thing we have to remember."
says my friend, after a pause,
"Is not to get fixated on the destination."
"It is the journey we take to get there
that is more important."

And with that my friend disappears
as quietly as they arrived.
With only an empty mug as testament
to their presence at all.
Above me the dance in the sky continues,
regardless of whether I view it or not.
It dances for the one that designed and made it.

*I have been trying to find a name/term to describe this sort of poem that I write and I've come up with the term "micro-story".*

*The inspiration for this one came during one of our "Encounter" worship nights at my church and it got me thinking about the wonders of the world around us and how God creates such beauty and then gives us the ability to appreciate it.*

*We all go through tough times or lean periods in our walk with God. During these times I find it a great help to just take time out to enjoy what I see around me. It was during one of these times that God spoke to me about our individual faith journey being more important than the final destination. He uses all our previous experiences and we will probably never know how he has used those fleeting interactions we have with people we never see again. In the same way that we are all unique so our experiences with him and the journey we take with him are unique.*

*Yes the journey may be difficult at times but he never leaves us to journey alone.*

# QUIET OF NIGHT

The moon blinks its way onto the world.
The clouds part and the countryside below
is cloaked in its soft silvery light.
Edges are no longer sharp but rounded.
Life is much softer.

A quiet descends.
Sounds that are usually masked by the
shrill and busyness of the day
can be heard once more.
Far off sounds travel further.
Sound closer.

The peace of the night shouts at
you after the hectic day.
The clear, sharp air stings your lungs
as it clears them out.

Contentment is looking into
the heart of the fire.
To listen to its crackle and hiss.
Watching the shapes made by the
flames between the logs.

The fire that brings a pool of warmth
and light to those around it.
The fire that brings both security and peace.

This is what I see when I meet with my Lord.
The clouds of the day part.
The shouting, competing sounds of
the day are stilled.
The peace and warmth of your cloak envelops me.
Your loves clears and refreshes my being.

How refreshing and quiet is the night.

*This is one of my older poems that pre-dates the kick-start of my writing efforts in 2016.*

*The inspiration for this poem is the disproportionate amount of pleasure I gain from sharing a simple camp fire with friends. I think this is a pretty universal thing, there is nothing like simply spending time in the company of good friends staring into the heart of an open fire.*

*It was while doing this one evening that I starting thinking about how it mirrored the feelings I have when I make the time to be intentional about just relaxing in God's presence.*

# Stalked By The Black Dog

*Image credit – Jennifer Litts sdg*

# STALKED BY THE BLACK DOG

The Black Dog that tries to stalk me
has found me once again.
He tries to intimidate me by making
his presence known.
He wants me to know that he is there.
He wants to keep me looking behind.

To take my eyes off what is ahead.
To keep looking to what is in the past.
To try to make me afraid of the future.
To drag me back to the darkness of before.
To tempt me to walk deeper into the bleakness.

But in this tunnel of loneliness,
this tunnel of one person's walk alone.
This tunnel of subdued light,
of grey walls and ceiling, there is still light.

Periodically along the walls are studded
the pointers to a route of escape.
Low lighting banishes the darkness in lipid pools,
with one pool leading to another.

Illuminated arrows point the way;
Towards a way of easy escape.
As does the dim glow of coming daylight
in front of me that invades this space.

So do I stay paralysed?
Rooted to the spot looking backwards?
Or do I look forward to where my light comes from?
To my own personal coming dawn?

Do I keep placing one foot in front of another,
acknowledging the dark but refusing
to be consumed by it?
Acknowledging the dark thoughts
that try to ensnare my mind.
To preoccupy it, to occupy it fully?

But I cannot deny the light that beckons me forward.
Cannot deny the half-whispered words
to keep on walking.
So walk on I shall in the sure and certain hope that
full daylight will appear once more.
That the sun will rise once more.

The Black Dog may try and stalk me.
To drag me back to his world of dark and hopelessness.
To remind me of all that I have done wrong.
All that I have failed at.

But the coming daylight of the dawn that
precedes the rising sun reminds me
that even better things are still to come.

So I continue.
One step in front of another.
Moving forwards.
Towards the rising sun.

---

*During the past few years there has been a growing acknowledgement here in the UK about mental health issues, particularly among men. This has encouraged a really healthy debate about mental health and a much better understanding of it and how many people are impacted by it.*

*One of the campaigns that I've become aware of is the "Black Dog" one and it's encouragement that it's good to talk about mental health issues and that it's "OK" to not be "OK" (www.dancingwiththeblackdog.com)*

*I have had my own minor mental health issues in the past and continue to have to be aware that I can very easily become a "glass half-empty" type of person, particularly if I'm tired and/or stressed. When I'm in this place is often the time the Devil will come alongside and try and tell me all sorts of rubbish. It's at times like this that I really have to work hard to keep focussed on God and follow his direction. It really is a case of walking in what I know of God's character rather than follow what I am feeling.*

*Yes, I still have my "dark" days and sometimes these merge into a longer period. I know that when I'm in this place I'm not a "fun guy to be with". However, I also know that God is right here with me going through it alongside me. I also know that it's perfectly acceptable to tell people around me who I trust that I'm not "OK". They will still love me, support me and encourage me forward. I just have to hang on to God, try to ignore the lies the Devil is trying to get me to believe and keep moving forward with God into his purposes for me. Some days it really is about just putting one foot in front of another spiritually.*

# WELCOME HOME

The wooden shack stands on the shore of the lake.
Half in, half out.
Supported on its stilts it is neither of
one world nor the other.
It bridges between worlds.

Across the raised wooden walkway I step.
To transfer from the land to the lake.
Planks creak beneath my feet as I
walk towards the front door.
Locks creak and the door swings open.
Light floods in.
It catches the swirling dust that glints
like tiny stars.

At the back of the shack extends the balcony
that appears to float above the water.
The deep, blue, silent water.

Here I sit drinking in the sun,
the water,
the scenery,
the trees,
the quiet.

The silence stills my soul.
Striving ceases and peace returns.
Now the quiet things can be heard once more.
The still small voice inside.
The whisper outside.

The light wind moves amongst the trees.
The leaves rustle and they make their quiet ssshhhh.
The wind moves the water, ripples appear.
I cannot see the wind.
But I can see its effects.

Now that peace has returned and
activity has quietened I can hear it once more.
The wind of the Spirit.
I turn my head and feel it brush past my face.
In an instant it is gone.

The evening arrives, welcomed by lengthening
shadows and golden hues.
The waves on the lake subside and it returns
to a mirror once again.
The cliffs opposite burst into golden light
reflecting the sinking sun.

I feel guilty for just sitting and watching, listening.
There is so much to do, things to be done,
activity to complete.

I go to move to engage in these activities but
instead hear the question
"Why do you make to leave?"
I answer "I have many things to do Lord;
Many jobs to complete."

"So you have; But will you not stay a while longer?
To sit and enjoy each other's company.
To tarry a while, to be at peace.
To enjoy a moment of rest?"
I sit back down.

Sometimes all God wants us to do is to do nothing.
To simply rest with him.
To spend time together.
To enjoy his world together.
To be together.
To listen together.

His love is not dependent on
the tasks we do for him.

*The inspiration for this came whilst visiting the C3 Church in Cambridge UK (http://www.thec3.uk). While I was waiting for the service to start projected onto the big screens in the main meeting auditorium was a picture of the shack I've attempted to describe along with the text "Welcome home".*

*God really "arrested my attention" with both the picture and the text. Over the coming weeks it refused to go – until I sat down and wrote this poem.*

*For me it linked with what had happened to me at Newday 2016. On a number of occasions, on different days, while I was singing during the worship God asked me to stop singing and just listen. I have to admit that I did find it strange to stop singing and just listen to the worship and to God.*

*So it is this theme of not being afraid to simply stop and spend time with God doing nothing that this poem is all about. It also touches on the fact that whilst we live in the world we are no longer of the world.*

*It is so easy to get wrapped up "doing stuff" – both spiritual and domestic that we can lose sight of the fact that God wants a relationship with us. He wants to spend time with us. He wants to listen to us. He wants to speak to us.*

# The Causeway

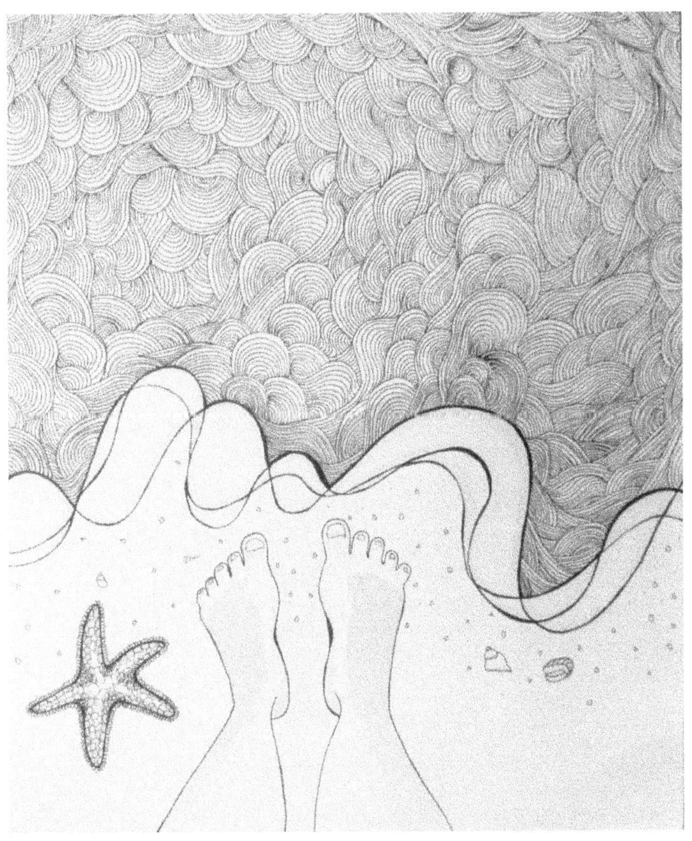

*Image credit – Jennifer Litts sdg*

# THE CAUSEWAY

On an island midst the sea she stands.
Around her the blue-grey labyrinth of
walls and gates extend.
High walls that all but exclude the sun.
Deep shadows do they throw.

There are places where the sun cannot shine.
The chill of these places reaches to her bones.
She pulls her cloak tighter.

Walking around this emplacement she senses others.
Hears muffled footsteps echoing off the walls.
Catches fleeing figures through the corner of her eye.
But she sees no-one; interacts with no-one.
No contact.
No touch.
No words.
No love.

But to her this feels familiar; safe.
She has grown up in it and
it has grown up around her.

She walks to the open main gate and looks out.
The emplacement is an island,
but it stands only a short distance from the mainland.

She looks out on green fields and woods opposite her.
On sun-soaked fields and trees
gently moving in the wind.
The small white houses dotted around the hills.

Sometimes the sound of voices and laughter
get caught by the wind and are wafted
over the sea to her.

But there is a divide.
A fast-flowing deep blue water
separates her from this land.
Stout poles mark the edge of the
causeway that links the two.
Around each pole extends a sizeable wake,
so fast does the water flow.
Even at the lowest tide the causeway is invisible.
Always there, but always covered.

Little does she know that the water is shallow.
The speed,
the flow,
the colour,
the temperature
make it a thing to fear.
But still she feels drawn.

Slowly she walks through the gateway,
down the path to the causeway.
Walking away from isolation towards
warmth and light.
At the water's edge she stops.

The way-marking poles stretch into the distance.
They mark the safe passage,
but one that cannot be seen.
One that has to be taken on faith.
The waters brood around each pole.
She cannot see how deep the water will be.
Still she feels drawn.

From here she can see people on the mainland.
She can hear their voices.
She stands transfixed for a moment,
not knowing whether to go forward or back.

Then a warm breeze catches her hair
and she hears the whisper
"Come; Trust; Do not fear".
She drops her cloak from her shoulders.
With courage she takes a step into the frigid waters.
They encircle her toes.

A step of faith into the unknown.
Little does she know it,
but her journey of faith and love has begun.
Begun with one small step.

# Bio

*I was almost not going to write anything extra about this poem but leave it to each reader to come to their own conclusions.*

*I admit that this is a very allegorical poem based on a number of pictures God gave me which when put together made this story.*

*Suffice it to say that all our journeys into a personal relationship with God started with a single step of faith.*

*In many ways the last year has been a "journey" for me too. A journey rekindling my desire to start writing poems again and (even more scary for me) sharing them openly with others. Partially this has been a journey of obedience in that I have started to act on what I feel God is telling me to do rather than find excuses not too.*

*On this journey over the past year I have been greatly encouraged by a number of individuals who all happen to be called Jo. So I dedicate this poem to Jo M. Jo. J. and my own Jo. Thanks for all your encouragement, please keep holding me to account!*

# The Lonely Poetic Journey

And so the pen meets paper once again.
Its thin black trail moves across the page
leaving its indelible trace behind.
Curves, lines and dots join together into
something that communicates.

The curse of the blank page that cries out
and taunts me is slowly eroded.
The inner voice of comparison dares me to stop
'Who will want to read this!'
And so its companion, self-doubt comes and
joins the party forming about this page.

Do I have a plan for where this will go? - No.
Do I know where any of my writing will end up? - No

Instead, tightly screwing up my faith in
he who calls me once again to this
adventure I set forth, never knowing the outcome.

Even now I want to stop.

But my doubt and fear are overcome
by my awe for he that talks to me.
There are times I almost want to
cry out for the pictures and images to stop.
They come so fast I cannot track them.
I'm afraid I might miss something and lose something.

But if I were to follow this reckless path
of serving self, I would miss out on the
great adventure that lies ahead.
Because my eternal creator Father has
not called me to walk this path to
then lead me over a cliff.

To lead me out of my comfort zone, maybe.

Does this mean that my unwelcome guests who
meet me on this page now leave me alone?
No – I write despite their presence.
I choose to listen to that still, small
voice that whispered two sentences into
my ear all those years ago.

The one who talks quietly but with all the
power of the waves that have crossed the ocean.

So, after years of ignoring his requests,
ignoring the small voice calling to my soul,
I eventually caved in to him.
I wrote once more of what I saw and felt.
As I wrote so more whispers and pictures came.

So am I now some sort of 'Super Saint'?
Absolutely not.
Often everything inside me wants to run away.
To close this notebook and file it safe away.
To stop.
But I know that if I was ever to try and hide it,
the book would follow me and find me.

Yes, I have a choice.
I can choose to walk away from this adventure.
But, even if I just think about it, I can hear
the disappointment in His voice.
In my spirit.

He will not prevent me from leaving,
for he holds me with an open hand.
But I can hear the silent tears.

So, I take his hand once more.
"I don't like this road we are travelling" I confess.
He smiles and replies
"I know – but I am with you – take courage!"

There may be times that I really feel
that I travel on my own,
with few physical friends around me.
The irony of the loner feeling lonely
does not escape me.

In those times of doubt, I simply remember the
lengths he went to search me out.
To pay a blood-debt that was not his.
To re-establish a friendship I was not even seeking.
He did not do all this for no reason.
There is purpose, even if I cannot discern it.

And so I shall meet my unwanted companions
around a blank page once more.

*As Creators we can all have our "off days". Those days and/or times when we doubt what we are doing or think what we are producing is of little value.*

*This poem is the result of one of those such times I had recently. A time where I felt so creatively alone within my home church that it almost physically hurt.*

*However, through the preparation I had put in to a small group we are leading I knew and know that what I am producing is of value. I may rarely see the reaction of those who read what I write but that does not devalue what I produce. Everyone has a unique creative expression that needs to be expressed so that everyone benefits from seeing and aspect of God from a slightly different perspective.*

*Yes, I still have my inner critics telling me to stop writing. They have not gone away and they most certainly have not stopped shouting at me. But is choose to continue pressing forward despite their best efforts.*

*If you are a Creator who is struggling – please don't give up. We need your unique contribution.*

# Juxtaposition, Synchronisation

The following two poems are presented in different forms. One with a male voice and one with a female. You get to choose which one applies to you.

This is such an intimate poem that I think it needs to use the correct words that reflect the gender of the reader.

# Juxtaposition, Synchronisation
## (Male Voice)

This is something I do not want to write.
I want to turn my back on it.
To look away.
To close the door.
To walk away.
I do not want to go here.

But your hand compels mine.
Wherever I turn I see you.
You gently remind me of what I need to write.

Write about the struggle within me.
The struggle between head and heart.
The struggle between the truth I know,
and how my heart feels.
How I feel.

I know I am your son.
That I have been fully adopted into a new household.
The old has gone.
The new has come.
But how I feel is tainted by the model I had in life.

I know I am imperfect.
But all I tried to do was to show love.
To demonstrate that there is always forgiveness,
no matter what I have done.

Freely have I been forgiven of much.
Freely I forgive.

To extend the hand of love and acceptance.
To make the offer to walk together across
the bridge of love into the new land beyond.
One where the past is acknowledged,
but not allowed to colour the future.
To build on a new hope.

Inwardly I feel rejected.
Passed over.
Set aside.
Replaced.
Expunged.

And here is my struggle.
What I know in my head but
feel in my heart are in conflict.
My eyes read your word and see the
truth of how you see me;
your heart of love toward me.
But my heart still feels the pangs of rejection.
Of being treated as if nothing.
How I wish I could feel your arms around me.
To hear your words of love.

Half of me wants to stay hidden.
To work away behind the scenes.
To avoid the spotlight.
So here I work, in the half-light of the background.

But you are not content with this.
You send your son to seek me.
He finds me.

Where could I possibly hide from him or you?
He calls me by name and by relationship.
"Brother come with me. Our Father wants us."
With his guiding arm about my shoulders
we walk together.

From the dimness of backstage to
the light of front of house.
In front of many people my Heavenly Father
hugs me and calls me by name. My name.
He turns to all those present and announces
"This is my son.
He conducts business in my name."
So fully have I been adopted.

Before all those present he acknowledges me.
In the midst of the marketplace
he affirms our relationship.
Something that did not happen in life,
has been affirmed in the heavenly realms above.

Oh my Father, help my feelings synchronise
with the truth of who I am in you.
Help me understand what it is to have
a Heavenly Father who fully accepts me.
Help me consign the past to the past.
To leave things of the past in the past.
To look forward and not back.
To look to the hope of the future,
not the disappointment of the past.
To know and feel your loving embrace.

Through all that happened you were there.
Help me to remember the good.
To forgive the things that are past.
To let them go and accept your love and care.

It is finished.

# JUXTAPOSITION, SYNCHRONISATION

(FEMALE VOICE)

This is something I do not want to write.
I want to turn my back on it.
To look away.
To close the door.
To walk away.
I do not want to go here.

But your hand compels mine.
Wherever I turn I see you.
You gently remind me of what I need to write.

Write about the struggle within me.
The struggle between head and heart.
The struggle between the truth I know,
and how my heart feels.
How I feel.

I know I am your daughter.
That I have been fully adopted into a new household.
The old has gone.
The new has come.
But how I feel is tainted by the model I had in life.

I know I am imperfect.
But all I tried to do was to show love.
To demonstrate that there is always forgiveness,
no matter what I have done.
Freely have I been forgiven of much.
Freely I forgive.

To extend the hand of love and acceptance.
To make the offer to walk together across
the bridge of love into the new land beyond.
One where the past is acknowledged,
but not allowed to colour the future.
To build on a new hope.

Inwardly I feel rejected.
Passed over.
Set aside.
Replaced.
Expunged.

And here is my struggle.
What I know in my head but
feel in my heart are in conflict.

My eyes read your word and see the truth of
how you see me;
your heart of love toward me.
But my heart still feels the pangs of rejection.
Of being treated as if nothing.
How I wish I could feel your arms around me.
To hear your words of love.

Half of me wants to stay hidden.
To work away behind the scenes.
To avoid the spotlight.
So here I work, in the half-light of the background.

But you are not content with this.
You send your son to seek me.
He finds me.
Where could I possibly hide from him or you?

He calls me by name and by relationship.
"Sister come with me. Our Father wants us."
With his guiding arm about my shoulders
we walk together.

From the dimness of backstage to
the light of front of house.
In front of many people my Heavenly Father
hugs me and calls me by name. My name.
He turns to all those present and announces
"This is my daughter.
She conducts business in my name."
So fully have I been adopted.

Before all those present he acknowledges me.
In the midst of the marketplace
he affirms our relationship.
Something that did not happen in life,
has been affirmed in the heavenly realms above.

Oh my Father, help my feelings synchronise
with the truth of who I am in you.
Help me understand what it is to have a Heavenly
Father who fully accepts me.
Help me consign the past to the past.
To leave things of the past in the past.
To look forward and not back.
To look to the hope of the future,
not the disappointment of the past.
To know and feel your loving embrace.

Through all that happened you were there.
Help me to remember the good.
To forgive the things that are past.
To let them go and accept your love and care.

It is finished.

I don't usually edit my poems much, preferring to write them up pretty much as I have received them. However, there are always exceptions to rules, so this poem is an edited version of the original poem. It represents the version I read at the Newday festival.

For the past few years I've been part of the team taking a small group of the young people from our church to Newday. Whilst preparing for Newday I felt God tell me to take some of my poems with me. I printed off a number and put them in a "camp proof" folder. However, God kept bringing me back to this one with a "that one too please" message so, eventually, I printed it off and placed it at the very back of my folder never intending to read it.

During the festival I was able to read a number of my poems during the Open Mic slots run by The Lounge. Throughout the week I kept feeling God prompting me to read this poem. I did not want to as I felt it too personal to read to an audience. However, come the last day of Open Mic slots I just knew I had to read this so I edited into to the version you see above and read it. I felt very, very nervous and was not sure I would make it through the whole poem. However, I did and it seemed to touch a cord with a number of the people there so I felt I had to "save" this version. I've had to do this edit from memory as I ended up giving away my original version at Newday to someone who asked for a copy

If you, like me, are one of those who struggle to understand God's father relationship to us and with us because we don't have a particularly good earthly "role model" I hope this helps.

# THE VOYAGE

As I sat with my back to my low, whitewashed croft
little did I know what was to unfold.
Enjoying the warmth of the sun, I thought
my days for adventure were over.

Then a gust of wind came from nowhere
and caught my attention with the scent of the sea.
My eyes alighted on my boat moored
at the edge of the shore.
Lightly bobbing atop the clear azure sea
it tempted me to get excited once more.

And thus the voyage started.
Tentative at first I hugged the shore,
kept land in sight, navigated the slight swell.

But the voice called me out into the deeper waters,
into the unknown.
So I turned the dragons head of my boat out to sea.
To the horizon.

Immediately the wind strengthened
and snapped at my sail.
The dragon's head rose up and snapped at the wind.
My boat surged ahead and I clung on.
White water curled around my bow and then
left a trail so clear behind me that
I felt I could easily turn around and
follow it back home to safety.

It was easy in the sun, revelling in its warmth.
But presently the dark clouds of doubt and fear
gathered before me.
I wanted to turn back, but the wind drove me on,
it was too strong to withstand or fight against.

So further and deeper I went.
Into a new sea of deep indigo blue capped
with many white horses riding huge waves
that tossed me about like so much flotsam.

Then darkness and rain enveloped me.
I could no longer see where I was going.
But still the wind drove me on,
becoming stronger and stronger.

Fear overtook me.
I was sure I was going to join
Neptune in the depths below.
To feel the wave's deadly embrace as they
drew me down into their realm.
In desperation I lashed myself to my steering oar,
buried my head and waited for the inevitable.

But still the dragon's head stood tall and proud.
Unbowed it pointed a way forward,
eluding to a faith that far exceeded my own.
The storm deepened and obscured all light.
It battered me from all sides.
Relentless.

Exhausted I waited for my inevitable fate.
To be consumed.
To let darkness envelope me in its heavy cloak.
However, the voice and the wind
had a greater faith than my own.
They had a plan that would not be thwarted.
And, as the earth rotated beneath me,
the sun did indeed rise again,
spoke to the storm and dismissed it.

It would be many hours before I became aware
of the sun on my cheek once more.
Its gentle caress broke into my darkness and I awoke.
My fears had not been realised.
The dark place of solitude.
Somewhere not desired but
somewhere that still has to be travelled through.

Most times this is travelled alone,
the dark pilgrimage of the soul.
A traversal of faith to the hoped for
better, brighter place.

A place that is currently unseen, not even on the
horizon.
It is literally a place of faith.

Somewhere that is hoped and yearned for
even though currently unseen.

Somewhere the heart knows exists
even though the eyes perceive it not
and the mind starts to doubt its existence.

Because even after the deepest, darkest storm.
when rain and tempest seem to strain to
rip apart and destroy, the sun will eventually reappear.

The storm will abate and pass.
Its strength will diminish and eventually be exhausted.

Opening my eyes once more I saw
the unbowed dragon's head.
It continued to point the way forward.

Looking beyond it's open mouth, I saw a
smudge of land once more.
Security and a new hope perhaps?
But as I looked harder the land in front of me
was unfamiliar – almost alien.

The voice, the wind and the sun had
decided that my days for adventure
were not yet over and behind me.
So I accepted their lead and went forward.

---

*This poem has a bit of a strange history.*

*I initially wrote it during one on our local Burn-24/7 meetings. At the time it seemed rather different in tone & mood to what we had been experiencing during the extended time of worship.*

*Like everyone else, little did I realise what the next 18 months were to bring.*

*Covid-19 came and overnight our worlds contracted to the walls enclosing the space we lived in. Time spent in the close proximity of friends and colleagues became replaced with a more distant, virtual existence. Time spent chatting over a hot drink with others was replaced with solitary times watching the kettle boil at home. Life, for many, was reduced to an existence where simply surviving was the goal.*

*For many this started a voyage into a terrible storm and into many really dark places. Mental health suffered greatly. Friends and family were taken from us without the chance to say any final "Goodbye". Many mourned alone for so many things.*

*When I first wrote this I simply filed it away unsure if I would ever publish it. It just felt so different, unfinished almost. Something with a bit of a learning towards the old Anglo-Saxon chronicles.*
*And so it sat, gathering virtual electronic dust in my laptop.*

*And then, out of the blue God prompted me to write a few stanzas during one of our Sunday morning (virtual) church services. I'm trying to get better at writing when God prompts me as, for me, it is a valid way of worshipping Him.*

*After I had committed the words to paper (yes, I'm a rather "analogue" person in that respect) I thought "Interesting, but what do I do with them?". It was at that point that God reminded me of this poem.*

*So, re-reading this poem from a post-pandemic eye and adding in those new stanzas I see that it now has a new life. A new life that means it is time it was published. And so it shall.*

*Image credit – Jennifer Litts sdg*

# PARADISE LOST

As much as I want to escape it,
Paradise lost begins with me.

No matter how many excuses
"It's not my fault because…".
No matter how many comparisons
"I'm not as bad as them!"
Paradise lost begins with me.

With every cutting, unhelpful word
both spoken and thought.
With every time I rush by,
too important to listen to you.

For all the times I put me first and push others down.
For all the times I choose to ignore compassion.

When I think I have all the answers.
When I use my words to pull down
rather than to build up.

When I judge others more harshly than I judge myself.
When I look at what is external and not the heart.

As much as I want to hide it,
Paradise lost endures due to me.

When I think that I can fix all things.
When I think I have no need of others.
Paradise lost endures due to me.

When I exclaim "Look at what they get away with!"
When I want to help "sort out" others
rather than starting with me.

When I think I can strike a bargain with God.
When I think that God is impressed
with what I do for him.

When I think that I can do anything
to restore my broken relationship with God.
When I think that perfection can share a space with me.

When I love because they first loved me.
When I love for what I can get in return.
Paradise lost endures due to me.

In truth, I can do nothing.
I am truly lost.
I was the one who walked away.
I am the one who closed the door.

Paradise is lost to me.

*This poem came about as a result of the monthly poetry challenge instigated by a poetry group I go to. This month the challenge was to write a poem inspired by Milton's Paradise Lost as we were going to have our meeting in the cottage in Chalfont St. Giles where the English poet & parliamentarian John Milton lived from 1665 to 1667.*

*As you know, I'm no English scholar so I thought it a good idea to read Milton's Paradise Lost before trying to write anything of my own. Then I found out that it extends to 12 books! I did not have time to read them (and 17th century English requires quite a bit of concentration) so I looked into the themes around Paradise Lost and its companion piece Paradise Regained.*

*I then approached my version of Paradise Lost by looking at it from a far more personal angle; how we are all responsible for losing our own version of paradise by what we think and do on a daily basis.*

# THE GIRL AT THE WINDOW

The yellow light streaming from the window
drew her forward.
The warmth of the light in strong contrast
to the cold and grey outside.
The grey that had become her companion,
her life, her bed.
Hugging the shadows she edges forward,
not wanting to be seen.

Feet that had long since lost their
feeling shuffle forward.
Numb fingers stretch out.
She edges closer to the glass.
She wants to look inside but not to be seen.
To be an invisible witness.

She sees a family busily setting a table.
An open fire crackles.
Voices rise and fall.
Plates clink.
Cutlery clangs.
Laughter abounds.

Even though the chill of the cold seeps
into her fingers, her toes, her nose,
the warmth of the room is almost projected outside.

Tears silently form and overwhelm
the dam of her eyelashes.
Silently they descend her cheeks,
leaving little tracks of clean skin.
Silently they fall to earth, like so many of her hopes.

Inside the room a child stops and
looks out of the window.
Looks straight at her.
Holds her gaze.

She recoils away,
wanting to disappear back into the grey.
To furl her cloak of loneliness ever tighter about her.
To feel its familiarity envelope her once more.

To disappear.

The child inside leaves the room.
They make their way through the house
and opens the front door.

The light streaming behind the child makes her blink.
She is not used to looking into the light.
To look up.

Wordlessly the child looks into her moist eyes,
smiles and extends a hand.

She is transfixed.
Rivers of tears flow down her cheeks once more.
She takes a step forward but stops.
The warmth is alien to her.
Uncomfortable.

The child walks out from the doorway.
Moving from the warmth and light
into the cold and grey.
The hand remains extended.
The gaze remains locked.
The smile remains welcoming.

She moves forward and her hand is
entwined by the child.
Fingers interlocking fingers.
Across the threshold she steps.
Steps into a world long since alien to her.
A world filled with chatter.
Voices.
Warmth.
Love.

She is gently guided to a chair at the table.
A chair set just for her.
Coat and hat and gloves are removed.
Food appears.
Conversations and chatter roll about her,
inviting her to be included,
but with no weight of expectation.

All this time the child sits beside her,
hand in hand.
Finger still interlocked with finger.
Still with a smile.
Security.

And so the slow process of acclimatisation
to a new normal starts.

Silently the front door is closed by unseen hands.
The cold and grey is shut out.
A new normal is entered and embraced.

*Recently I hosted/facilitated (not sure of the correct word to use) our mid-week small group meeting. Over the preceding months I've been very challenged/exercised to explore ways to bring different creative expressions into our worship.*

*I've been particularly encouraged by the blog from Bethel Church in Redding California (Created to create ) and by groups encouraging us to use more than just our voices in worship (e.g. We Are Set Sail – where faith meets art). So this week we dived in and spent the whole evening using different creative expressions of our worship to God. We had drawing, painting, writing, origami and crochet! At the suggestion of someone else in the group we had backing music but it was music only – no words.*

*It was in this context that I wrote this poem, based on a picture I've had for about 6 months. After I shared it with our group someone asked "So who's the girl then?". My honest answer is I don't know.*

*When I write I sometimes get a sense of who the characters are, sometimes not. However I think that this is just my view at the time and I don't want to "get in the way" of anything God may be saying to other readers by clearly saying "and in this poem character X clearly represents Y". Rather I think that the characters in the poem will mean different things to different people at different times.*

*This poem could be about a journey into faith or about how God provides families for those of us who don't really have any (see Psalm 68v5) or it could be something completely different. Just read it with an open heart and mind and see what God says to you.*

# MASQUERADE

Even among her circus friends she was an enigma.
Softly spoken she moved with such grace,
but no-one had ever fully seen her face.

She wore her hair long so that it
acted as a veil to be drawn across her features.
Combined with a hat she was ever anonymous.

The woman with no back-story, no past,
she had just appeared one day.
But was accepted for who she was nonetheless.

Her stage persona was even more enigmatic.
The full flowing dresses she wore coupled with
the renaissance mask that girdled her head gave
little hint to what lay within.

The mask that covered her whole face,
placing it forever in an enigmatic half-smile.
Only her eyes gave the slightest hint
of the depths that lay within.

When not performing she invited those attending
to meet her to have future mysteries revealed.
The irony of the woman with no past
telling them of their future was lost on them.

There was nothing unusual or outstanding about
the man who entered her tented pavilion one day.
Nothing that would make anyone take a second glance.
Nothing in the way he looked.
Nothing in what he chose to wear.
Nothing in the way he carried himself.
Just ordinary.

She invited him to sit down in front of her
and offered to tell him of the things to come.
As he turned his hands up and offered
them to her she stopped.
Such unusual scars.
She was reminded of her own.
It was as she took his hands in hers that
the assignation took a completely unexpected turn.

This time she saw not his life but her own.
Snapshot stills of a life she now hid
flashed through her mind.
A visual timeline of her life,
going oh so far back.

She recoiled, gasped and dropped his hands.
Disconnected.

And now the tables really turned.

His hands now gently took hers.
Gently drew her back to the table between them.

No longer frightened, she now felt strangely secure.
She raised her eyes and looks into his face.
"I think it's time you stopped hiding." He says.
With great gentleness he reaches behind her head.
Unties the ribbons that holds her
exquisite mask in place.
Quickly she puts her hands up to her face
to keep the mask on.
"I can't" she whispers.

Again, with great gentleness,
he takes her hands once more.
Slowly he draws them away from her face.
Her mask falls away, still cradled in her hands.
He looks full on her face and smiles.

"You are beautiful" he says softly.
"But my scars.... they are ugly" she stumbles.
"Not ugly, rather a testament to
old battles fought, and eventually won."
"I see beyond the surface, beyond the obvious,
to the heart within".

Time now stretches in this shared peaceful moment.
Neither felt the necessity to rush away.

Eventually she found her voice and asked
"What do I do now?"
Without answering he stands up and extends a hand.
"Simple. Follow me."
"No longer does your past own you".

Laying her mask on the table,
she follows him out of her dark pavilion.

*This poem was written during a virtual mini-Burn meeting over a Zoom video-conference call one Friday evening. Due to the Covid-19 restrictions in force at the time we could not meet face-to-face.*

*Over the past couple of years, I've been experimenting with and becoming more comfortable with writing as part of my time of worship. I still enjoy sung praise and worship but at the same time I'm very open to interrupting things and prompting me to write. So, during the extended time of worship that the Burn-24/7 setting presents I always have my notebook to hand so that I can jot down any thoughts I may have. Yes, you can interrupt your worship to have a conversation with God!*

*As the evening progressed my notes coalesced together to the theme that would become this poem.*

*Towards the end of the meeting we were given space to bring any prophetic words, pictures etc. and someone spoke about people wearing masks and being prepared to let them go. I just love it when God gives the same picture/inspiration to multiple people in a meeting especially when they almost word for word say the same thing!*

*So, this poem is all about letting go of any masks we may have built for ourselves. Anything that prevents us from showing who we truly are to those around us – especially to our close faith friends. These masks may be beautiful and well-crafted, but God wants us to come before him with nothing between us. That is his eternal plan. He knows all about us, the good and the bad and yet he still loves us with an everlasting love. One that will never reject us but rather accepts us where we are and invites us to walk with him into a better tomorrow. Lucy Grimble () summarised this so eloquently in her introduction to her song "Don't Hide" on the album "Lucy Grimble live at Burgess Barn":*

> *"When we come before the father we don't have to hide any part of ourselves, that the original design of our relationship with father God is naked and unashamed – nothing hidden. We don't have to perform, we don't have to pretend with God and I think all of us in a sense are looking for that in life. We are looking for spaces where we can just be ourselves and just be safe and be known."*

# My Stance On AI

First, please be assured that the content of the poems in this book is proudly "human authored" content. No Generative AI has been used to create the text within the body of the poems.

I'm not a luddite (well, I hope I am not), but I just don't think there is a place for AI when it comes to creating content that relates to the lived experience of life and the emotions that go with it.

We have made the occasional use of AI-based tools to assist us with things like spelling, grammar etc.

The artwork that illustrates some of the poems is also completely human authored. No AI-generated images have been used alongside the poems.